The
ABC'S
of Parenting

Great Quotations Publishing Company

Written and Compiled by Dr. Anthony P. Witham
Edited by Debbie Hansen
Cover Art and Design: Jeff Maniglia

© 1992 Great Quotations Publishing Company
All rights reserved. No part of this book may be reproduced or transmitted in any form or by any means, electronic or mechanical, including photocopying, recording or by any information storage and retrieval system, without permission in writing from the publisher.

Published in the United States by:

Great Quotations Publishing Co.
Glendale Heights, IL

Printed in U.S.A.
ISBN: 1-56245-062-X

Lovingly dedicated to my daughters Lisa and Carol, my stepchildren Tara and Michael and my grandchildren Stevie, Derek, Lauren, Andrea and Pato Jr. all who serve as constant reminders to practice more than preach the suggestions contained herein.

Parenting is a difficult job with lots of responsibilities and demands! Yet if we can approach these tasks in positive ways, parenting can also be filled with joy — in the love we receive from our children, in the privilege of sharing their energy and laughter, and in observing the ever-wondrous process of their growth.

Each time you open **The ABC'S of Parenting,** we hope you will find some insight or inspirational thought which can help you become a more sensitive observer and caregiver of those who love us most and crave our "Gifts of Time."

>   Anthony P. Witham Ph.D.
>   President, American Family Institute
>   Valley Forge, Pennsylvania

Accept the individuality of your child — when others engage in comparisons.

*A*s parents, we never stand so tall as when we stoop to help our children.

The most beautiful discovery family members make is that they can grow separately without growing apart.

*M*essages to children lose their impact when they are stated repetitiously.

Especially with children, small things wear the garments of greatness. The little words "I love you" and "I'm sorry" enrich both the giver and receiver.

*I*f I were starting my family again, I would laugh more at myself, my mistakes, my failures. So many of the tensions of life arise because we take ourselves so seriously.

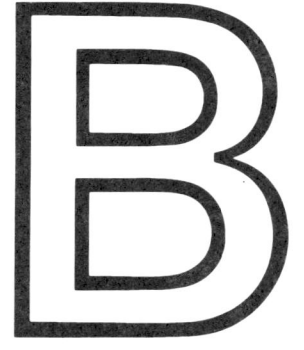elieve your child — when others fail to work at establishing mutual faith and trust.

*B*uy your child a diary (with a key) and keep your promise never, never to peek.

With children, just the touch of the
hand, a loving smile, a careful
compliment, a close caress,
can work wonders.

*T*he best games of children are timeless
and there seems to be nothing more
natural than play.

*W*hen parents make it easy for children
to behave well, their self-esteem grows.
They learn to see themselves in a positive
light and feel successful in being
able to please us.

*I*t is only in childhood that quality books can have a deep influence in shaping lifetime values and interests.

ompliment the smallest efforts of your child — when others can find only fault.

*T*oo much love never spoils children. Children become spoiled when we substitute 'presents' for 'presence'.

Ask your child which school subject is most frustrating and how you might help.

*R*emember, our children need our love and support the most when they deserve it the least.

*I*f there is anything we wish to change in
the child, we should first examine it and
see whether it is not something that could
be better changed in ourselves.

C.G. Jung

*P*robably no other thing encourages
a child to live and love well
than sincere praise.

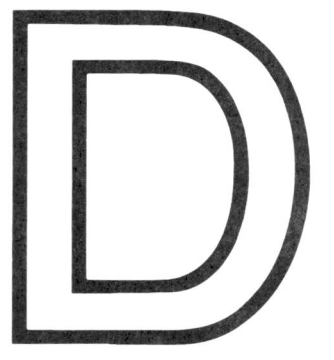iscipline your child — when others fail to establish appropriate limits of behavior.

*T*each your child how to make his own decisions and to accept the consequences of his behavior.

A family discipline program should help children feel proud of themselves through acquiring greater self-control, leading to good feelings about oneself.

*D*on't make a long speech when a stern
glance or brief comment is all that's
needed to get your message
across to a child.

*F*orgive and forget once discipline has been administered.

"We all make mistakes. Let's try and learn from them".

Self-esteem is built brick by brick with kind words, and compliments.

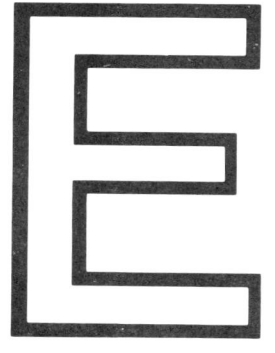njoy simple things with your child — when others are missing priceless moments and memories.

*T*here is an addictive quality built into the TV set. The more children watch, the more they want to watch.

*O*ne of the great memories you can give your child is to attend and applaud your child's performance at school.

*C*hildren spell L-O-V-E . . .
T-I-M-E.

*G*ive your child the kind of love you dream of receiving.

It's children that pull us toward love and it's our everyday chores that pushes us away from them.

Forgive your child — when others cannot seem to forget mistakes.

*D*iscipline is one of the clearest and most frequent expressions of love between parents and their children.

*C*hildren don't require great amounts of parental time and attention — but they thrive best on a steady supply of short and long stops along the way.

*T*oday, just stop what you're doing and look at your child more intensely.

*V*isit a hobby store and encourage your child into a lifetime hobby.

*A*ll of life is learning,
but childhood learning relies on
a once-in-a lifetime openness:
A belief in people and in things.

Greet your child with a smile — when others prefer wearing frowns.

*G*ifts Of Time Our Children Ask Of Us . . .

RELAX with me . . .
and make me feel comfortable being with you.

DISCOVER me . . .
and learn what makes me different from the rest.

LISTEN to me . . .
and hear what really concerns me at the moment.

PRAISE me . . .
and observe the power of a simple compliment.

DISCIPLINE me . . .
and teach me the importance of self-control.

READ with me . . .
and nurture a lifetime of love for books and libraries.

PLAY with me . . .
and enjoy the little things that make for lifetime memories.

STUDY with me . . .
and model for me the joy of lifetime learning.

CREATE with me . . .
and help me discover my special gifts and talents.

HUG me . . .
and remind me often of how much I am loved.

PRAY with me . . .
and help me reflect on how I can make this a better world!

*E*very child needs to feel that he or she is the only one of his or her kind.

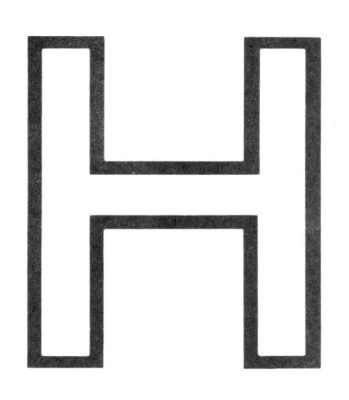

Hug your child — when others underestimate the need and power of touch.

*O*ur love for our children must not hinge on response.

*T*oday, jot a loving thought down and tuck it in a place your child will find it.

A hug is the perfect gift.
One size fits all.

*F*urnishings and fireplaces accent the beauty of a house — tender thoughts and touches accent the beauty of a home.

A parent becomes old when he shuts his mind and stops learning from and with his child.

Studies suggest that it takes four positive statements from a parent to offset the effects of one negative statement to a child.

Imitate the simple faith and optimism of your child — when others prefer to grow in cynicism.

Next time the phone rings when you're really enjoying your child, let it ring.

*I*t is important to accept your children as individuals with distinct personalities, capabilities, and needs.

Avoid labeling your child as careless, slow, or messy.
Children have a way of living up to the way you may see them.

Remember, the well-attended child
aims to please his parents,
not frustrate them.

*T*here is no other thing
that is more important for the
future well-being of parent or child
than the deep love of
father and mother for each other.

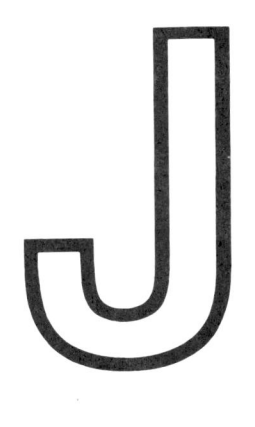

Joke with your child — when others have lost the ability to laugh.

*I*n every real man a child is hidden who wants to play.

— *Friederich Nietzche*

*O*ut of the mouths of our children come
words we shouldn't have said
in the first place.

A laugh at your own expense
   costs you nothing.
   Lighten up today.

*L*ove and Discipline cannot be separated. They are inseparable partners.

*P*arents who enforce obedience are caring for one of their childrens' most basic needs.

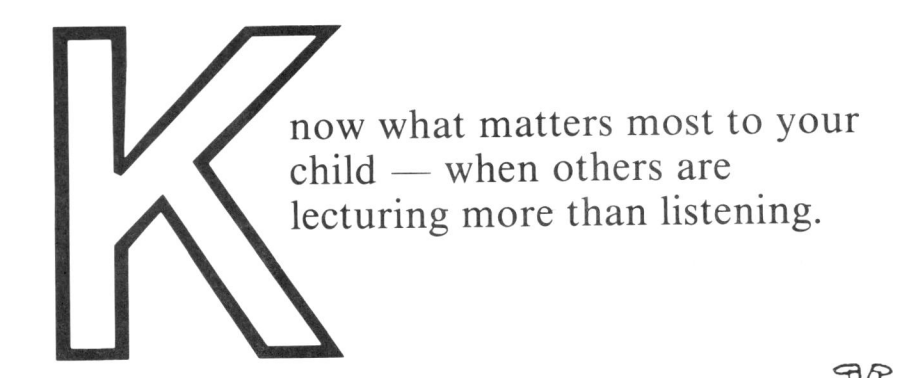

Know what matters most to your child — when others are lecturing more than listening.

A parents' actions are the picture book
of his values.

*T*he foundation of all good behavior in children is a child's sense of being noticed and being loved by his or her parents.

*N*ever mind about tomorrow our children plead: For it's *today - this moment* - that we need.

*F*or children, what I hear, I forget.
   What I see, I remember.
   But what I do, I understand.

*E*very child needs parents who agree
on the rules and boundaries that guide
the child's growing.

Love your child with daily expressions of affection — when others forget to say "I Love You".

A healthy family is able to express affection openly. Words such as "I love you" are an important part of daily life.

*A*s parents communicate, solve problems, share power, love and express compassion — they are leaving indelible impressions on their children.

*T*he greatest gift parents can give their family is a healthy marriage in which the parents act as role models.

*I*t is estimated that the average child asks 500,000 questions by the age of fifteen — a half million opportunities for parents to share something about the meaning of life.

*P*arents must be well-disciplined themselves before they can demand the same from their offspring.

Model appropriate behaviors for your child — when the actions of others can serve to confuse.

*C*hildren discover who they are by first having it defined for them who their parents are, and who they are not.

*T*he great man is he who does not lose his child's heart.

— *Mencius*

*Y*our child's reaction to your style of
discipline is of far greater significance
than the method you may choose.

*Y*ou can always tell a home with a five-year-old in it. You have to wash the soap before you use it.

*C*hildren can never receive too much praise for jobs well done or for appropriate behaviors.

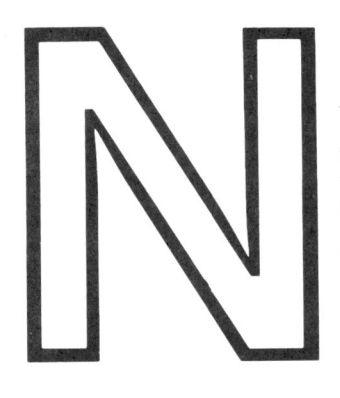

Nurture the creative potential of your child — when others can overlook the special gifts of childhood.

*T*he child who can be found alone with a cherished book has already learned that education doesn't demand a teacher or a classroom.

*V*isit your library or book store and
return with some of life's
greatest treasures.

*L*et your child know that you don't take for granted the little things they do such as making the bed without being told.

*I*nstead of buying toys that "do" — or "perform" — give children a few basic things and let their imagination do the "performing".

*L*isten to your children today whatever
you do or they won't come back
to listen to you.

Observe classroom progress through your child's schoolwork — when others show little interest.

*T*ry to get your child to keep a reading diary; besides giving him or her a sense of accomplishment, it will be a memento in later years.

*I*f homework and high grades become diamonds in his parents' crown, the child may unconsciously prefer to bring home a crown of weeds that is at least his own.

*W*hen you speak with your childs' teacher what words does the teacher use: Problems and needs, or talents and accomplishments.

*P*arents who are truly interested in lifelong progress for their child will encourage rather than exhort. They will take their direction from the child.

*W*hen your child is kind, unselfish, helpful, creative, industrious — say so!

Pause and have fun with your child — when others are too involved in their yesterdays and tomorrows.

*D*on't regret that you can't give your
kids the best of everything.
Give them the best of you!

*J*ust being silly with our kids can be one of life's great pleasures.

The only things children wear out faster than shoes are parents and teachers!

Pity the child who is hurried and spanked into bed. Bedtime is such a great opportunity to build a loving feeling of belonging.

A good marriage is more important in raising our children than excellent parenting skills.

Question the amount of time you spend with your child — when others offer "presents" rather than "presence".

*T*he richest child can often be found in
the lap of the poorest parent.

*T*he best toy is one the child creates.
Take your child outside and show him
how to build forts out of sticks,
make boats out of paper —
the possibilities are infinite.

*P*arents remain a child's first and most
impressionable teacher. No one can give
or nurture love and good feelings
quite like a parent can.

*C*hildren don't waste precious time with the past or the future as we do. They rejoice in the present — as we should.

*C*hildren are more likely to talk with adults who take them seriously.

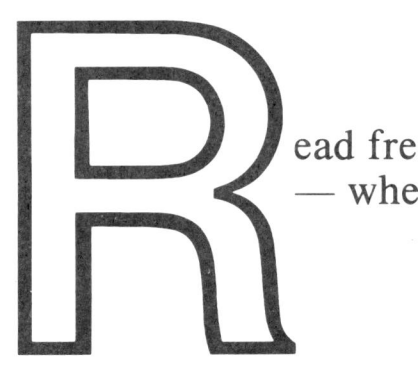

Read frequently with your child — when others prefer television.

*K*eep puzzles, games and building toys near the TV. Kids may become involved and ignore the TV.

*L*imit the amount of TV your child watches. Too much TV watching results in stress from emotional overload.

*N*o entertainment is as available as reading nor any pleasure so lasting.

*O*ften just telling children what you heard them say will encourage them to keep talking.

Study and grow with your child — when others have chosen to stop learning.

*C*ontact your child's teacher this week
and let the teacher know you're interested
and available to give that
extra encouragement that may
be needed at home.

Have your child record each day's homework assignments in one notebook and show it to you. This helps in the "I've forgotten my homework at school" excuse.

*R*ecord some favorite books on tape so your child can "read along," or simply listen, when he or she is too tired to make the effort to read.

*P*arents who live well, laugh often and
love much with their children,
have discovered the keys to success.

Don't use an allowance in place of your time or to "buy" love.

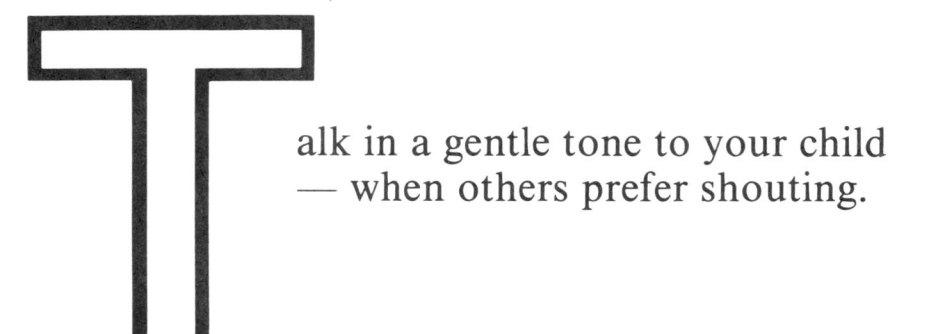

Talk in a gentle tone to your child — when others prefer shouting.

*C*ommunication in the home is not improved by loud speakers.

*R*esearch suggests that nothing influences children's value systems more than the relationship they observe between their mom and dad.

*A*lmost all household chores help a child learn to follow directions and carry out activities, an important foundation in building character.

A parents shout is aggressive but non-assertive. It's an expression of frustration and an admission of powerlessness.

*D*on't criticize your child in anger.
You'll usually overreact.

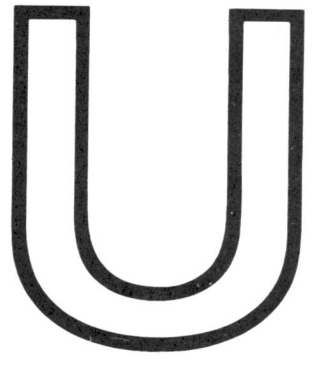

Understand and nurture the traits you wish for your child — when others fail to give such values any serious thought.

*C*hildren are always ready to play games. Often it's the parent who must be given the extra push — the one who needs stress-free moments the most.

Of all the things parents wear before their children, their expression will always be the most important.

*H*elp your child find better solutions to his difficulties; don't solve the problems for him. Remind the child everyone has problems and everyone makes mistakes.

*I*t is important to accept your children as individuals with distinct personalities, capabilities, and needs.

*L*augh a lot together! The healing power of laughter has long been recognized as an effective antidote for stress.

Value the time you share alone with your child — when others underestimate the need for such intimacy.

*T*onight, review your childs' schoolwork and show your interest in his progress and efforts.

*L*et your children open up the junk mail this week and decide what to do with it.

Spend time talking with your child in a way that he or she understands, in terms and values that have meaning in the child's life.

*W*hen we invest time, kindness and interest in each family member we have created memories that will never sleep.

Build in your home a balanced climate of laughter, adventure, surprises, mutual care, good music and books.
Make it fun to live there.

Work toward appreciating small successes with your child —when others meet only frustration in seeking perfection.

*C*hildren are a precious and priceless gift to ourselves and to our world and they deserve our love and nurture.

*S*hare relaxing moments with your child. Stop to watch a sunset, examine a flower, admire a birdsong.

*P*oint out and applaud your child's improvements, no matter how small. He or she will learn to be optimistic.

*I*n praising our children we often overlook the flowering and less obvious skill for living: Kindness and caring, honesty, and a sense of humor.

*P*arents who have learned to listen well are not only popular with their children, but after a while they know something.

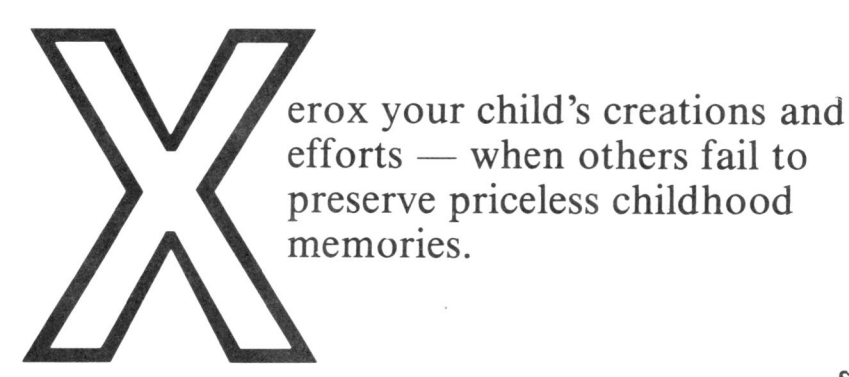

Xerox your child's creations and efforts — when others fail to preserve priceless childhood memories.

*F*rom the beginnings of life, what children learn is grounded in what parents teach through the example of how they choose to live.

*L*abel your child's photos with names, dates, occasions. You WILL forget.

*Y*our child's attitude as well as his achievements are worthy of praise.

*O*ne of the great pleasures of life reserved for parents — to have a child offer a hug and an "I love you".

*C*hildren are the best source of information about themselves. If we take the time to notice and to listen, we'll discover what's needed.

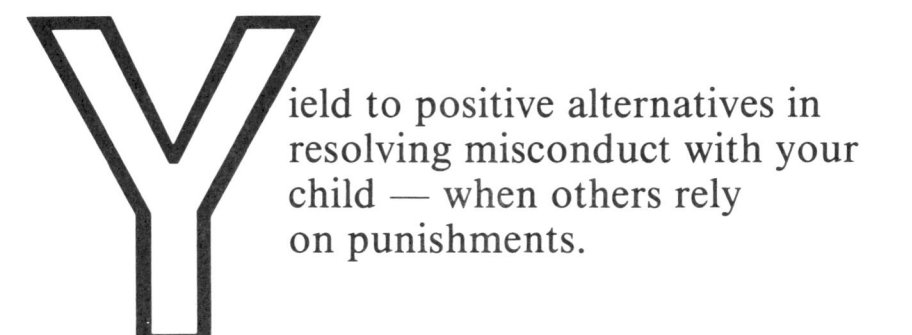

Yield to positive alternatives in resolving misconduct with your child — when others rely on punishments.

*P*arenting can be more fulfilling when positive words are used in training a child, negative methods such as slapping and yelling drain energy and make parents feel irritable.

A family discipline program should help children to live more peacefully with us, reducing the reasons to shout.

*P*arents who enforce obedience are caring for one of their children's most basic needs.

"No man can possibly know what life means, what the world means, what anything means, until he has a child and loves it."

— *Lafcadio Hearn*

Remember that the "teachable moment" for your child is immediately following words of praise.

Zero in on your strengths as a parent — celebrating the positive differences you are making for a better tomorrow.

DISCOVER ME

Each child brings to this world
    a special person to be **discovered** -
    a special potential to be **realized** -
    a special talent to be **shared.**

No one else
   can ever be this **person** -
   achieve this **potential** -
   or sing this **song.**

These unique gifts have been
   entrusted to each child
   of the universe —
And will remain **hidden
   treasures** until we
   encourage their
   discovery and
   delight in their
   offerings.

A.P. Witham 1987

A family discipline program should
help children to please us
more than aggravate us.

*C*hildren who fear their parents often become deceptive — they learn to lie in order to escape their restrictions.

Defending the Moment

Never mind about tomorrow - our children plead;
For it's today — this moment that we need.
There are no other moments that really matter -
"Now, mom! Now, dad!" they chatter.
Each minute must be guarded -
making the most of the here and now.
It is today we must treasure —
right now . . . somehow.

A.P. Witham

A happy home is not one without problems or disappointments, but one that handles them with understanding and love.

*M*ake a habit of recording in a special notebook the funny, profound, or otherwise memorable sayings of each child.

*C*hildren from an openly affectionate family feel wanted and loved. They feel good about themselves and about others.

*W*hen disciplining, always provide a way for your child to retain his or her sense of value and dignity.

*E*ven the child with good feelings of self
is going to say "you don't love me"
once in a while.

*L*ightening our hearts through childlike play allows us to loosen up and enjoy our days rather than endure them.

*H*is heritage to his children wasn't words or possessions, but an unspoken treasure, the treasure of his example as a man and a father. More than anything I have, I'm trying to pass that on to my children.

Will Rogers, Jr.

*C*hildren are a gift. Treat them well.
Do your best for them.
That's all any caring parent can really do.

ABOUT THE AUTHOR

As founder and president of the American Family Institute at Valley Forge, Dr. Witham has initiated the Gift of Time Campaign of Family Renewal in partnership with the public and private schools of Pennsylvania.

The 'Gift of Time' program of renewal is presently outreaching to 500,000 families through schools and agencies committed to strengthening and enriching the family unit. Over the past 10 years, he has organized community tribute programs honoring over 30,000 parents, teachers and caregivers of children and addressed more than 500 audiences, seminars and conferences.

If you would like to inquire about contacting Dr. Witham as a consultant or speaker, please call us and we will be happy to forward you additional information. Call us toll free at 1-800-354-4889 or AFI at (215) 269-4100.